Transitions

Elizabeth Carson

Dedication

This could only be dedicated to my late husband, Michael, who was the first reader of all my books and was never other than encouraging.

I miss you, Love.

Table of Contents

Invitation

On each page, a poem.
Behind each poem, a mystery… and an adventure.

Let me invite you in.

Where might this compact set of words take you?
Will you find yourself traversing
highlands of enchantment,
desperate bogs of despair?
Will you find home truths, or simply home?

Laughter may accompany you, or tears,
a strip tease or words so dense
there's no excavating their meaning.

Or perhaps there is no journey at all,
merely a comfortable certainty that you are
exactly where you belong.

Take a deep breath and come on in.
Don't be afraid. A poem is, after all,
just words.

Let's travel together,
explore the magic woven through the rhythms,
agree, and argue, and learn.

You are welcome. Come on in.

Part 1:
An Expected Death

Neighborhood Walk

We were drawn outdoors into sunshine
for what proved to be our last walk... well, shuffle really,
your legs contesting once familiar movements.

It was a balmy afternoon, not too hot,
the world ripe with summer
as we navigated the sidewalk.

Our pace was speedier than had become usual.
I was encouraged...
until, that is, I realized.
Caught in forward momentum, you had lost
the strength to hold yourself back.

We didn't talk much,
but I gripped your arm,
partly to keep you upright,
partly just to hold on.

Neighbors waved. You always were popular,
and they all knew it couldn't be long.

Our last walk...
    Last... last...

A Day in July

Today, the day you died…

After, it was the thought I'd never see you again
that got to me,
Never again look at your face
    I'd studied for a lifetime.

When they came to take you away from me
I wanted to block them, say No, it's too soon,
But what would be the point?
Your physical self – your remains, how terrible a word,
    and how true –
was already changing,
no longer a part of who you had been.

It's up to memory now, that perilous vessel,
clinging to the you of forty years ago, twenty,
    yesterday.

Today, the day you died, I am numb.
Don't go, love. Don't leave me alone.
Stay somewhere safe and whole,
somewhere I will know to find you.

Day 2

If asked, I'd say my current state
is bewilderment.
Turns out I'm not clear on the technicalities
of how to mourn,
especially in light of all that went before...

It seems I've been mourning for a long time.

Now, awash in this hollowed-out place,
I can't locate the germ of grief,
the weight of tragedy that is supposed to follow
the end of our life together.

I can't find anything, other than a mundane craving
for a grilled cheese sandwich,
a compelling need to make lists.

Don't rush, they say, plenty of time, but
what else should I be doing?

Deal with the funeral home,
return medical equipment – which means driving,
        and am I *compos mentis* enough to drive?
        Is it proper? Is it done? Do I care?
Commit events to government forms, change the accounts,
the ownerships,
all the minutiae of an ended life.

I almost said, ended existence, but that's not accurate.
You won't cease to exist for a long time.
Your presence hasn't let go. Will it? What is your timeframe?
For now, what I know is
you no longer occupy this odd, empty place
where our life is supposed to be.

Driving through Town

I felt so odd, conspicuous,
as if I'd tied a sign to the bumper
like the ones that say Just Married,
only at the other end:

Look at her, she has changed!
Her husband's dead! *Dead!*
She's a widow!
She's *different!!*

Different indeed.

Merely a woman going about her business,
as the day carried on without acknowledgment
of the tectonic shift in me.

Sunday Walk

I thought I was ready.
What I hadn't counted on
was the blankness of leaving for a walk with no one to tell,
no one waiting for me to come home again.

What I hadn't counted on
was passing couples – three today –
older, like us, and holding hands, like we held hands,
and smiling hello to my solitary self.

I smiled back and carried on,
but returned home frightened
by the insubstantial days ahead.

Anger

How dare you leave me alone?
How dare you?

But wait, I think. Be fair.

You did all you could to pave the way,
to make the business of dying straightforward.

But you couldn't tell me
what to do with the inheritance
of time alone.

Now I'm faced with the question
of how to navigate the days
when the scaffolding's been kicked out from under me.

There's a vacuum. No one breathes in a vacuum.

Ashes

Going to the funeral home, picking up your ashes…
I was all business, no tears.

That is, until I put the urn containing you
on the front seat of the car where you always sat,
    struggling with weakened limbs
     to get in, get out again…

I had to wait, to get a grip,
before I could drive away.
I had to convince myself
you weren't really there,
although of course you were.

Giving Voice

Though I don't cry,
some days can barely even talk,
why shouldn't I be able to scream?

One Month

You were watching, weren't you?
That first month, I talked to you constantly.
     Remember this, my love? Remember that?
     See what I managed, see what I got through.
It takes determination, dealing with life on my own,
Especially with my mind not functioning so well…

(And yes, don't fuss, I'm driving very carefully.)

I wasn't aware of you, exactly,
but still I talked.

Then, after that month, I woke one morning
and knew you were gone.

Was this my mind playing tricks,
moving into the next stage of widowhood?

I'd rather think you had been keeping an eye on things.

Wherever you are, I miss that watchfulness.
I liked the stability, the sense
of a rock behind me.

Because to be honest,
it's scary out here.

Erosion

How terrible it must have been for you,
who were so strong,
to lose dominion over your scarecrow body.

I'd awake in the night
to find you half in, half out of bed,
without the strength to lift your legs,
unwilling to disturb my sleep
and ask for help.

A Photo

Photos do you justice, always did, so here I see
a you I had almost forgotten,
smiling, with flesh on your bones
and a life to experience.

Aliveness is a strange construct
in the context of death,
and photos, however true, cannot capture
the flush of life beneath the skin.

Clearing Out 1

Yours, mine, ours,
and I get to sort it out.

All those years together… I've hardly ever experienced
living on my own.

Funny that the years have devolved into detritus,
a basement full of memories packed away,
filing cabinets storing the history of a family.

Perhaps the sorting
will reveal some inner order that is currently missing,
a way to make sense of what is left.

Nevers

Bedtime has changed.
A once simple, daily event
has new significance,
its value magnified
by absence.

Now I realize, all too clearly,
you will never kiss me good night again,
never give me that long cuddle
to carry me safely into sleep.

Bench

Your son is building a memorial bench for you.
Those walks, those times sitting on benches…
    he remembers.

This is your legacy, your most powerful legacy:
    our children,
strong and sure and loving us – loving you.

Anniversary Flowers

The blooms are almost gone
on our anniversary begonia, the one we gave ourselves.
Only a few flowers left.

But then, it's been over three months
since we celebrated our forty-ninth.

As the illness overtook you, we brought meals home
        from our favorite restaurant.
I set the table with our best,
        the begonia our centerpiece.
But you couldn't eat, the muscles refused to work.
Defeated, saying nothing, you waited for me to finish.

We acknowledged the day together as best we could,
on what we knew would be our last anniversary.

The begonia, my love, has lasted a long, long time.

Tears

I don't cry much.
It's my way, and I had months to prepare,
once it was obvious the disease had gripped you
and sapped, day by day, all you were.

No, I don't cry much.
But sometimes it overwhelms me, and I can't predict it.

I sit in the Federal Building, scarcely a sentimental place
with bland walls and cubicles and take-a-number-please,
and for no reason, no trigger,
I find myself welling up.

The Evolution of Stuff

Yesterday, our son took home your birding binoculars.
I don't know if he'll take up birding,
but maybe this is how things evolve.
What we loved changes hands, is reinterpreted
to meet different realities.

Two Months

Crunch time.

The work of death is done,
accounts changed, will updated,
house and car in my name only...
and now to get on with the rest of my life.

Easy, right?

But how?

My mind switches from overloaded to foggy.
After the first weeks of depleting busyness,
non-activity soaks me up,
leaves me without purpose.

Purpose kept the grief at bay.
Its lack points to a truth I'd rather not face,
not yet.

I wait, impatient, for my life to fit me again.

Meals

I cooked lamb chops for supper.
Lamb chops fled my life years ago
        (and yours, too)
when you couldn't eat them anymore.

Oh love, I feasted on those chops,
and the sweet accent of mint jelly.
Should I feel guilty for this small,
unshared indulgence?

Responsibility

Facing facts, it's all on me.
If I mess up, no one will rescue me.
If it breaks, it won't get fixed unless I fix it.
If I triumph, there's no one to cheer my success.
If I can't be home, there's no one to feed the cats.

If I scratch the car, miss an appointment,
forget to pay the taxes,
choose a poor investment, rip out the garden,
overshoot the budget…
it's all mine to deal with.

I'm out there on my own now.
Support, encouragement, comfort –
those died with you.

Difference

The difference, you see, is
    you died in my arms.
Who will be there to hold me
when my turn comes?

At a Loss

If I am not a caregiver,
Then what am I?

I'm not so good at excavating emotions.

One is there, though:
    Anger.

I'm not sure what I'm angry at.

At my age, I am free but no longer young,
screwing up my courage to be...
    What?

Some might envy me,
sitting here on a sunny morning,
time my own.

But the reality is, I have no idea
    what to do
    With this new void.

Five Months

It's Christmas, and you're not here.
I mean, not anywhere,
        no hint of you.
The tree of celebration stands lit and lonely
across the room.

In fifty years, we've never been apart
for Christmas.

The night is ripe for haunting,
ancient chant in stone cathedrals,
unconnected to electric light and heat on demand,
unconnected to anything
in the known, glossy world.

Hearing You

Did you know our children asked me
not to change the message
on the voicemail?

Not that I don't hear your voice in my head,
as if you'd never left, but
it's the only physical print we have now
Of the sound of you.

Six Months

Winter rain drenches the windows.
Songs of the Auvergne paints a tinge of longing on the air,
our cats groom each other by the fire.
Lights as small as tears ripple over the mantle,
       Relics of solstice recently past.
My world is steeped in melancholy beauty,
Soothing my restless mind...

Patience.

Soon enough I will be clear again,
soon enough understand my own strengths.

I feel I should pay homage to myself,
my emerging, solo self.

I honor both, my lost love and my unbound soul,
As I hover on the edge, not quite ready to run free.

Support

I'm not alone. Please don't think
I weather these days alone.

It would be possible to focus entirely
on family and friends and activities,
and not deal with the rest of it at all.

No. Scratch that. I'm kidding myself.

It's got to happen,
the emptiness,
the specter of memories,
the fear.

It's not right to slough them off.
These times are a part of it.
I live them, and live through them,
and in a funny way
I am grateful.

Alone

Definition of *Alone*: the flu, and no one
      to take my temperature,
      bring me juice,
      Put cool washcloths on my forehead.

I tell myself, it's only flu, I'm not dying.

(And anyway, why should dying scare me
      when you and I have lived your death?)

I tell myself, of course you can drag yourself up,
      feed the cats,
      wash your sweaty body.
I tell myself a dozen things.

What I can't tell myself
is where you are when I need you.

Clearing Out 2

When nothing else calls,
there's always tackling (again!) the basement storage.

What a pack rat you were.
how much you relied on cardboard boxes.

Our thought patterns never ran in parallel,
so it's no surprise
the boxes make no logical sense to me.
Several held rags. Why so many rags?
Two held trash.
Some were stuffed with clothing, likely forgotten.

Wiring, light bulbs, shoe polish...

Your mind on occasion was a mystery.
I remember all too well
how you kept things, just in case...
not to mention your tendency
to never replace them where you got them.
Is it any wonder I bought – and hid –
my own set of tools?

And so to the challenge, switching the basement
from your thought patterns to mine.
I get to decide
what is treasure, what is junk
and how it should be organized.

(Perhaps we'd agree on the rags...?
No. We wouldn't.)

I kick start my logical mind
and dig in.

It's a way to occupy the afternoon
and probably should have been done long ago anyway.

Lessons

However painful, I can't say
your dying has been without its lessons.

Bluntly put, you wanted to go.
And I struggled, and still struggle, to understand.

I cannot imagine, yet,
a world without me in it,
or me without the world.

To know what matters, to accept
dying as a natural part of living...
I'll get there, take your example to heart.

It helps that you have led the way.

Coming to Terms

I'm walking away from an old life,
because I have no choice,
leaving behind what I must leave behind
without you to create the alchemy
of our marriage.

You were always such a presence.

Oh, love…

Nine Months

You might approve, or you might not,
but I've made changes.

Some small, the shifting of a chair,
banishing the old encyclopedia to a box in the garage.

Some larger, creating a writing place
from the small bedroom,
made personal to me.

And I found a picture – you'd remember it –
of you, sailing on the Lake of Two Mountains,
hiked out, silhouetted by the sun.
I've hung it in the bedroom, a private place
for things like memories.

Remnants

It's all dribs and drabs now,
Days when I scarcely think of you,
others when, unexpectedly, you're back full-blown.

Not, I admit, what I expected of mourning.

It's a process, as all that went before
finds its rightful place
in my new, sparkling life.

One Year

Our children came to honor you.
We walked to the site you'd chosen
        in the woods,
I recited a poem,
and each in turn, we consigned you
to the land you loved.

Then we returned home
for our own, private celebration.

We ate big squares of cheesecake – your favorite dessert,
        the one I made for our fourth anniversary,
        back when it was just the two of us,
        and reprised every year since.

So, as I say, we ate cheesecake,
and listened to Beethoven's seventh –
        engrained in our family's collective psyche –
and talked.

We spoke of you, memories of you,
family memories,
comfortable together.

And our children spoke of their children,
their lives so different from ours,
    so far away.

You would have loved it.
It would have suited your style in every way,
our family united,
the most perfect wake.

A Last Farewell

And now, my love, I have said goodbye,
released you, and consigned you
to the earth you loved.

Go now with an easy heart.
Be well, be safe,
Godspeed.

Requiem

By Robert Louis Stevenson

Under the wide and starry sky,
　　Dig the grave and let me lie.
Glad did I live and gladly die,
　　And I laid me down with a will.

This be the verse you grave for me:
　　Here he lies where he longed to be;
Home is the sailor, home from sea,
　　And the hunter home from the hill.

This poem haunted me almost from the first, when I
stopped by the bridge to watch the ducks and it came
flooding into my consciousness. I could never have
found better words to honor your final rest.

Part 2:
Transits and Everyday Happenings

A New Face

I'm adjusting to this face,
now that the old one's disappeared into a maze
        of sags and right turns,
        and fair enough, a few wrong turns, too.

The pressure's off,
and it's time to test that old saw
        about earning your wrinkles.

I study this face and see –
        Surprise! –
        I see potential.
The grooves chart paths to new adventures,
to things not experienced... yet.
To the exquisite ordinary, the voluptuous unexplored.

I'm learning my new face.
Purple with a red hat is the least of it.
With every new, brave step
I explore the routes to treasure
in the map of my amazing, miraculous face.

Bindweed

The devil binds.
Bindweed climbs a fence, works along a rail,
        latches onto a tree,
its trumpet flowers beguiling
in the gentle morning air.

Bindweed doesn't let go. The devil is like that.
Its roots colonize the soil,
its stems wrap the post,
and all the while, its flowers seduce.

Can you name what binds you? Most can't.
Senses focus on satisfaction,
and never notice the tendrils
around the ankles.

Creation

Connection, creation,
hidden imperative
to draw a soul from slumber.

Seed, potential,
warmth and water
soften the shell,
a passage enabled.

Gestation, anticipation,
nurturing a miracle,
a seedling, a plant.

Fecundity, expansion,
stretching to sunlight,
parent of seed,
reveler in sunshine.

Releasing, allowing,
the cycle complete,
inevitable composting,
freedom to leave.

Corpse Pose

This is my body, the space I have been given
        to occupy, this time around.
Head, upper back, glutes and heels
anchor me to the floor.
The bridge of my nose twitches
with the memory of glasses.
My thumbs curl into my open palms
        like small animals seeking sanctuary.
I am heavy; I experience
my own weight upon the earth.

Releasing to stillness,
breathing slowly, with intent,
        connecting to all that is,
I grant myself this pause.

For ten precious minutes, once a week,
the neurons rest, the great sigh of completion
        is mine to know.

Angels

Dancing on the head of a pin?
Here's the question: Why?
But wait...

See them, if you will, like dandelion seeds,
radiating in all directions,
tiny feet pointed, toes barely touching the steel,
each in a white robe, swaying,
anticipating that moment of flight.

Ah, dandelions. Few so-called weeds
have such a bad reputation.
For a fresh perspective,
ask a child, seed head in hand, ready to blow –
    it's as good as bubbles!

Now I ask, was there ever anything
so angelic as bubbles?
Ethereal, impossible, they move with the air,
floating to destinations of the imagination.
Spend an hour on the lawn with a bubble wand
and remember.

And so, I return to those angels,
    poised on the head of a pin.
How many? Lots. But they won't be staying.
On cue, they'll fly away
to waltz, in realms of fancy,
on the shifting summer breeze.

The Call

Life moves forward with no particular attention
        on your part.
It's routine, the stuff that fills the hours,
your busy life.

And then, without preparation, everything shifts.
Perception turns a little sideways,
and you are flooded; the world drowns you,
pulls you under, forcing you to know:

You are. You ARE.

The moment, when you catch your breath,
is delicious.

Is this enlightenment? If so,
incorporate it, chopping and carrying.

And don't forget.

Cherish that moment, remember the way
your soul responded,
allow your deepest self to rise up,
        quivering,
to the brush of the infinite.

Done

For Margo

You know it's done
>when the threads are tied and snipped,
>with no regrets left dangling.

You know it's done
>when silence matters more than words,
>more, even, than the spaces between words.

You know it's done
>when your masterpiece is complete,
>and you lay it down
>and walk away.

Autumn in the Bog

Rosehips are the only polished things
        in the bog today.
Golden leaves have flattened to ochre,
trees and trails to a gray-brown monochrome.

Well, autumn hits that way sometimes.

Not given to drama, the flat sky
releases its load of icy drizzle,
speckling the trail.

Conversation

One challenging aspect of a courageous conversation:
you won't survive it the way you expected to.

The Dark Times

Samhain is past, and
these are the dark times,
when humanity clambers for the light.

But I don't.

Darkness feeds batteries neglected
by our frantic determination
to deny its place.
Let the dark dominate,
allow the sun its winter respite.

Come Yule, I will decorate the celebration tree
with the tiniest of lights,
a promise, a hint of glory.
I will revel in friends and feasts,
light and warmth on demand,
nudging the darkness toward spring.

For now, I want none of it.

The dark times are not to be shunned.
I open to the dark, its nuances and secrets,
I allow its mystery into my cells.

I emerge fortified into the transition of winter,
the anticipation of the softer days of spring.

Made

Sleek, that's the word,
    groomed and polished, she is.
I don't like to think
what the suit and shoes cost,
the effort behind the makeup,
the hair so perfect that even in the wind,
    she's immaculate.

Sleek, her wall of credentials, there behind the desk,
    framed just so,
    proving who she is.

Sleek all day, impeccably handling
    every situation.
She is perfect in her role,
fast track, all eyes are watching.

In the morning she eats toast, the barest hint of butter,
    no marmalade,
and watches the rain.

Leaves, Releasing

Prayers enter the air
as falling leaves,
liberated, without resistance,
from outgrown attachment.

Leaves litter the ground.
They release their hold on the old ways,
settling into a new reality,
not of their choosing,
but of their accepting.

Pandemic Benefit

A clerk asked me today if I qualify
for the senior discount.

I haven't heard *that* in a while.

I know why she asked. I wore my pink mask,
the one with multicolored polka dots.
All that youthful exuberance
would fool anyone.

Thanks to my wonderful mask, she saw only
the laugh lines (yes, they are laugh lines,
absolutely laugh lines!) around my eyes.

She couldn't see
how everything south of the nose
sags.

I agreed I qualify, there was no point denying,
and accepted my old-age reward.

Me, a senior? Need you even ask?
Thank you, Pandemic.
For a moment there
you made me giggle.

Be Longing

Be longing.
Be needy, be without. But be prepared
to explore the wilderness of dreams and lost intentions.

Be the one forgotten,
because whatever happens next,
you'll be going it alone.

No one said it was easy.
Be longing, but don't stop
until you exhaust your options.

Then comes the hard part.

Be longing. Be clear, and then be driven
by the glory of the outcome.
Scavenge courage
from wherever you can find it
and go.

Sentence

Sharing words is an act
of profoundest vulnerability.

Words in combination reveal,
or trivialize, or say too much,
or go on and on and on.

Words are a gift. They suggest, they pontificate.
Words create the atmosphere. Words convey truths.
Words lie.

Words form complex, intricate patterns,
clauses safely contained by commas,
gaudy adverbs, overblown adjectives,
prepositions for definition or obfuscation.

Words are a mirror, a passage
to comprehension. So wisdom grows,
after due consideration.

Actions, on the other hand,
require a more immediate response.

Names

The name of deity is not revealed.
God, for instance is generic, while *Venus* personifies.
Face it. Some things
we're not entitled to know.

In this (as in other things), cats are much the same as
deities.
      Just ask T. S. Eliot.
      Ask my cats.

What is it about names, anyway?
I've gone by several.
Those who have called me by one
reject the rest as unfitting
to the 'me' they know.

Furthermore, names convey no uniqueness.
My Elizabeth isn't the queen's.

So, let's leave it that a public name
is a convenient handle
pretending to capture an essence,
that 'me' I share with you
while keeping private my own,
ineluctable name.

Sext (Noontime)

Don't you love the articles
      in magazines and weekend supplements
      and (heaven help us) littering social media?

Easy to have healthy and varied lunches!
Exercise! Meditate! Get a good night's sleep!

Damn!

Take, for example, my lunch:
      crackers, a chunk of cheese
      (recently trimmed of mold),
      an apple.
Hey, it's food.

In mitigation,
assuming all goes according to plan,
(and need I mention that's a big if),
I'll go to the park,
      over near the bandstand,
where I'll listen to the wind for a while,
rambunctiously romping through
the treetops.

Tending

Mushrooms pop up all along the sidewalk,
mottling the grass.

I do not trust them.

I'll photograph, but never touch.
I am grown up, I have learned.

On the other hand…

I watch my grandson, not yet two,
pull red berries from a downed tree branch.
His pleasure is to throw them
      (ambidextrous, clever child!)
But what if my gaze should stray for just a moment?

What if one of those plump handfuls finds its way
      to his mouth?

Oh, mushrooms! How little we can hold safe
      our treasures.

Patience

It takes patience for flavors to meld,
The exotic paella, the mellow coq au vin,
    the flaky croissant
    with morning coffee.

Patience brings with it reward,
the measured pace of a bride down the aisle,
the depth of a prairie winter,
    yielding at last to the crocus.

Slow is a skill not easily learned
in a world of adrenalin
and instant gratification.

I rushed around, once. Wanted it all,
not tomorrow, now.

These days, I wonder why.
I find myself, as I age,
Content to relax into the day,
savor the most mundane of tasks,
the pattern of the vacuum on the carpet,
grooming a cat with long, slow strokes
    to the music of purrs.

This is fine.

Popular wisdom says the tranquil mind lives longer.
Maybe, maybe not.
But I do believe it lives more fully,
augmented by moments otherwise not noticed,
reaping the reward
of simpler enchantments.

Bee Magic

A bee bumbles by
and alights within the cup
of a squash flower.
The sun joins the party,
yellow of sun, yellow of flower,
yellow of stripes wrapping the bee.

The alchemy begins.

In perfect time, the flower births a squash,
warty, sundrenched,
yellow.

Add a stroke of kitchen magic,
and the squash unites
with the paler yellow of butter.

By a garden rich in bees and flowers,
in the mellow sun of late afternoon,
We dine on miracles.

Amok / Hapless

Today, faced with a dearth of inspiration,
I resort to an old trick:
open the dictionary at random,
spear it with a finger,
and build a poem from the word thus chosen.

This presupposes I can find a dictionary.

Failing, I resort online to Mr. Merriam and Mr. Webster,
and today's word, chosen for me, is *amok-with-an-o*.

It looks misspelled, this word.
Amuck-with-a-u looks righter,
and is in fact correct, although out of favor.
The online dictionary has a certain tut-tut quality about it
 as if to say
amuck-with-a-u is not quite the thing.

> (By the way, spell check likes *righter*,
> though heaven knows why,
> but not *wronger*, which somehow is more wrong
> than the comparative of right.
> Hmm.)

Now, where were we? Ah.
The written discourse rarely runs amok,
unlike a good conversation.
You start out exploring one concept,
and the words tempt you into quite another.
But if you fail to fully leave the first behind,
you've got muddied thought, aka muck. Mucky. A muck.

The word becomes its own definition.

Not content to leave well enough alone,
(see above on muddied concepts),
I consult an online newspaper source
which offers up a word of the day: *hapless*.

A funny word, that. Now, *hap* means luck. Once upon a
time
    (because *hap* is archaic, although *amuck*, alas,
    fails to attain such lofty status,
    having been in common usage more recently.
    But I digress…)
As I say, once upon a time one could have hap.
These days, is anything ever simply hap,
without the less?

How very sad, to be without hap…
It feels so non-specific, at a loss,
a lonely word in search of a home:
Good hap to you!

I'm hap-py to say
this hapless poem,
signifying nothing in particular, much less luck in
general,
is at an end,
having long since and truly run amok.

Covid-19, Spring 2020

In the anxiety-strewn night, I come face to face
with a new, or newly believed, reality:
this thing could kill me.

Momentarily frantic,
I am forced to acknowledge that I am, truly,
in the most at-risk demographic.
>   *What have I done?*
>   *Is it on my hands?*
>   *Have I breathed it in?*
>   *Dare I go out?*
Yes, this could kill me,

Home becomes a womb
in parallel with the threat posed by the world out there,
>   that innocent, new-green, familiar world
>   that used to be mine.

That doesn't mean life can freeze to a stop, however.
Once-a-week errands
>   (at odd hours, and only the necessities),
precautions that become habit.

When you're out in the world, it seems less real.
In spring, life surging in warm days
and people doing usual, human things,
it's surely impossible
that mortality is on the line.

Facts fail to line up. My mind is a muddle.

They tell me, in spite of the evidence of my eyes,
in spite of the burgeoning spring,
that illness lurks, death is a possibility,
and could be closer than I ever imagined.

Looking into the Future

In my mind, in a moment of scary precognition,
it's all vanished, the houses, the shops.
I stand on the opposite hill, looking out over my home,
and foundations have become scars,
trees sprout in erstwhile basements.

The roads that carried us
reduce to shadows through the trees.
My eyes follow the remnants, traces of routes
that still connect and intersect.

It's so easy to see what no longer is.
Imagination, of course, but...

We walk a dangerous path when we believe
what we have is permanent.
It would take so little
to end it all.

Greening

If you have a gown, my goddess,
a wondrous robe for special times,

That gown is green.

Chartreuse, teal, crayon from a brand-new box
in the hand of a first-grader,
all ripple in the breezes,
shifting, mutating with the varying light.

And around the hem – paintbrush red,
camas blue, palest cream of fawn lily,
reflecting yellow of buttercup.

You wear your gown with elegance.
It reveals itself gradually
to winter-blinded eyes. A shrub, a swath of grass,
a forest. The tips of branches, hints of yellow green,
will mature into the depths of summer shade.

The sweep of your gown
paints benediction on the land.
Your skirt swirls about you,
and we, all we who watch
as you create the spring,
rejoice.

Homeland

(On relinquishing the citizenship of my birth)

In your country I can walk with impunity,
and anyone might say to me,
"This is our country."

I look and sound the part, although
my nation-pride
finds a different home now.

Funny though. When I look in
from outside, I have a sense
of something gone askew,
because once I would have echoed,
willingly,
Yes! My country!

It's an unexpected hollowing
with roots in memory,
a lingering legacy
bequeathed by the land of my birth,
to the ones who leave.

Beginning

She heard a new word and asked its meaning,
then sounded it out: fab-u-lous.
The next morning, she remembered.

We made French toast.
She stood solidly on the step-stool and washed blueberries,
discarding the soft ones because her dad does.
She poked the tops of the eggs in the bowl
and remembered to hold with one hand
while she whisked with another
(and didn't spill a drop of egg).

When it was time to put the bread in the pan,
she soaked it well, then almost threw it
at the sizzling butter. I learned later
she had never before been allowed
this close to a hot pan.

She's five. In two months, she will be
in kindergarten. Life is a full-on exploration.
Loved and secure, nothing stands in her way.

Seventy years between us, but nothing else.
It's pretty neat, having a granddaughter.
You might say, it's *fab-u-lous*.

Why I Didn't Quite Finish the Book

Time for a break, a relaxing moment
to read our book club selection.

I prop my book on the arm of the chair
next to the plate holding my scone.
Cat arrives on my lap. I shove aside her tail.
I read three lines and bite into the scone.
Cat, sensing butter, reaches with a paw.
I raise scone and plate above my head with one hand,
brace the book with the other.
Cat eyes the plate,
a lodestone hovering on high.
Using a spare finger, I turn a page,
read three lines, then attempt to swap
the book for the scone.
The book falls.
Startled, Cat bolts
using claws in my thigh for traction.
I lower the plate, pick up the book, and resume.
Three more lines.
Cat returns, aiming for the arm of the chair.
I shove cat aside
and, getting there first,
cram the last bite of scone into my mouth.
Cat sniffs at my lips.
I read three lines and set the plate
on the table beside my chair.
Cat follows plate. I read three lines.
Cat returns to my lap, full of purrs, the predictable effect
of two tiny crumbs
scavenged from the plate.
I read three more lines. The purr is soporific.

After a while, I awake. The book is still there,
the cat is still there.
Three more lines and a glance at the clock,
and I am out of time.
I close the book, pick up the polished plate,
displace a displeased cat
and go do whatever I have to do.

It's good to set goals.
Tomorrow, I promise,
we'll read another twenty-one lines.

Inauguration

A peach-tinged sky makes a brief appearance,
before layers of impenetrable cloudscape,
scraped and shaped by the wind,
obscure its brilliance.

Those clouds deserve due reverence,
because all that radiance is a two-edged sword.
Once it pierces your own, personal night
you will be denied any possibility
of not-seeing, not-knowing.

Will you then bless or curse the break in the cloud?
Are you prepared to send forth your own light
to merge with all light,
and become part of a new dawn?

Ambition

There is, to say the least, a mountain in the way.
I'm meant to get across, or so I've been told.
Over there the sun shines brighter –
or so they say.

But getting there...?

The mountain casts purple shadows across the land.
The path climbs steep pitches
with few handholds. Stones to trip,
narrow ledges skirting canyons, where the next step
may – let's be honest – be the last.

But all that is ahead, not precisely here.
Here, at the beginning, the path is smooth,
winding through peaceful pastures and ripening fields
where blackbirds tune up for the day.
The sun shines as bright as it needs to, and hey,
a shadow is only a shadow.

What's wrong with this picture?
What ambition, what implication,
drives me to brave the tests ahead?
Who, exactly, guarantees greater bliss
on the other side?

Night Rhythm

Late night blues and brandy,
piano and bass are the air I breathe.

I am drunk on midnight freedom,
with myself in conversation—
in the depths of midnight I am real.

My body pulses to the beat,
the melody sets my heart to yearning.
Deep notes trigger a matching vibration
like fingers caressing my skin.
There's no escape
from the dark chocolate truth,
so bittersweet,
so satisfying.

It's coming home time.
At midnight, sharp sweetness on my tongue,
I relearn what's shoved aside in daylight
and give myself over
to where it will take me.

Autumn Rebirth

Where is the sadness in a forest of red and gold?
A pumpkin in its field, brilliant in crisp sunshine,
marks a transition, but never an ending.

Grieve summer's end? Not this woman.

Cooler winds and a warmer palette defy
the lingering somnolence of summer.

I embrace this deckle-edged glory, tease my senses
with portents.
So do I lay a foundation for the chill,
blanketed meditation
of winter.

Craft

The poetry of angst,
The tortured poetry of run-on sentences covering pages,
The poetry that eschews beauty in favor of hard-edged
truths...

This isn't my poetry.

Oh, I admire you
who craft the harsh words,
open your wounds to the world.

I'm not blind to the injustices, the crises
tackled in your poems.
But it's too much like work
to read them.

You might say mine is poetry for those
who got through it and came out the other side,
and now find value in watching a slug,
working its determined way
across the path.

Survival

The skills that allowed us
to gain a foothold on this planet
        are lost.
Is this sanity? Have we misplaced
forever the basics of survival?

Maybe. Probably.
Despite my emergency preparedness kit,
as I struggle through a one-day power outage
I can say with sad certainty, I would not
be one of the survivors.

The earth won't care if we do ourselves in.
In a decade, it will absorb whatever is left,
and those who remain will have relearned.

In a century, no one will remember
our remarkable progress.

Can't Win

Reflections on Francis Bacon's *Essayes and Counsels Civill and Morall*

Part 1

"Chaste women are often proud and froward, as presuming upon the merit of their chastity."

Well, thank you, Francis, for your high opinion
of womanhood.

Chastity is an old-fashioned word,
implying all the feminine virtues
including the obvious, nonnegotiable one.
But now it seems if I am chaste, I am, perforce, proud
by virtue of that very fact.

And froward? Really? Contrary and disobedient
because of being chaste?
Francis, whatever were you thinking?
Had you perhaps had an embarrassing encounter
with a saucy little number?
Or the queen?
> (Your queen, I mean, the first Elizabeth.
> Arguably (maybe) she was chaste.
> No question, she was proud
> and made rather a point
> of doing exactly as she chose.)
A froward queen for sure.

For the rest of us,
there's no winning this game.

Sigh.

Part 2

*"...it seems (though rarely) that love can find entrance,
not only into an open heart, but also into a heart well
fortified, if watch be not well kept."*

*... therefore it was well said, That it is impossible to
love, and to be wise."*

So, watch out, gents. That old devil love
can creep up on you, and you're toast,
however well fortified you are.

The object of your desire, if chaste,
is liable to be a handful,
and furthermore, she'll hold you back and bring you down.
you're pretty much condemned
to foolishness if not mediocrity.

A bad deal all around.

Part 3

"He that hath wife and children hath given hostages to fortune; for they are impediments to great enterprises..."

Should an intrepid man wade through
that muddle of chastity, frowardness, and pride,
succumb to love and claim a bride, pre-personal-greatness,
he's putting the kibosh on his prospects
(and doing his lady no favors either).

Yep. If he's got the gal, he's doomed himself
to mediocrity.
Unless, that is, the great deeds were done first,
and you, my dear, are a mere afterthought,
a kipper for his delectation.

Seems a man just can't think those lofty thoughts,
conceive the brilliant plans,
with a woman on his arm.
(I wonder where his thoughts have wandered off to...)

Of course, we women were incapable
of any thought at all, much less noble deeds,
in 1600.

And in Conclusion

Oh, Francis, how sad to caution
against women, against love and family.

Did you achieve joy?
I'm betting, not so much.

By the way, I can be froward,
and am exactly as chaste as I choose to be,
and have happy experiences of accomplishment,
even in the face of marriage and children.

I doubt you would approve of me at all.

Well, trust me on this, my dear man:
it's mutual.

Wind

A nasty November day,
    rain and wild wind.
I settle by the fire, content with books and tea.

Seven-Cat, however, is not content;
she chases the blowing leaves from window to window,
disturbed by the whistling in the chimney,
the gale rattling the pane.

She can't relax. Her hunting instinct surges.
She'll take on the tumultuous day, track it,
drop it at my feet with pride: *caught!*

As is right and proper. Seven-Cat is young.
She stalks life,
afraid she'll miss something
if she lets it drift by.

Aghast

Here's another word of the day:

Aghast.

Its very pronunciation evokes a gasp.

It's that 'gaa' sound, reminiscent of
the first sounds babies make.

Are babies born aghast at the scene they've entered?
Are they gasted by what faces them?

And yes, *gast* was a verb once,
as recently as Shakespeare.
Ghosts, for instance, gast, and we,
shaking and trembling,
flee to safety.

But do they mean to? The ghosts, that is,
do they mean to gast us?
Or are they just (poor things) lonely?

Gast, by the way, once meant ghost,
and this is getting nuts.
Now we have gasts gasting, and in reaction,
we, thoroughly and logically aghast,
put this odd poem aside
and like those haunted by gasts,
shaking and trembling,
get ourselves out of here.

On the Airwaves

It was just a white box with two knobs
on the table in my room.
It didn't work until the tubes warmed up.
This miracle box carried the voices, the music,
of the world.

It was all AM in those days.

On the radio in the kitchen, there'd be soap opera,
variety shows, evening dramas,
local news, Sinatra and Gogi Grant.
On my white box, I'd listen to Buddy Holly and the Everlys.

At night, there'd be Fidel on Radio Havana, WLS in Chicago,
other ghostly, unidentified voices,
all blanketed with static, wavering in and out,
but there, far away.

Now, the mystique's long gone.
I listen to FM, no longer hypnotized
by the open gateway.
Still, every room in my home
has its radio.

From the bedroom I can hear,
too faintly to parse words,
the radio chatter from the kitchen.
My mind welcomes the familiar sound
from decades ago,
an old friend come back to visit.

First Time Outdoors

As a kitten, intrigued, she leaves the security
of the room and steps outside.
The patio seems safe enough,
a familiar hardness under her paws.

But there's more. Tentatively
she reaches with a paw, touches the grass,
quickly withdraws.

The paw moves out again,
batting at the strange, prickly surface.

Intrigued, I remove my sandals
and join the kitten
at the edge of the patio.
In conscious imitation,
my foot brushes the blades of grass.

How long since I last allowed myself
this barefoot experience?

Inspired by discovery, the kitten frolics
and I do, too.
We stretch and roll, run races across the lawn.

Naming Song

Mountain, steadfast,
>   Meadow of snow and flowers.
>   Waterfall tumbles, landslide shreds,
>   And still the mountain stands.
Wisdom of mountain, saga of mountain,
Shelter of mountain, danger of mountain:
I am she.

Knit, interlocking,
>   A rhythm of clicking needles,
>   each loop needed, each loop governing
>   The fate of the whole,
The pattern cascades from my needles
in all its complexity:
I am she.

Mouse, whiskered explorer,
>   Curious, testing,
>   Nervous, darting,
>   slow to trust,
Care giver, shelter maker:
I am she.

Hands, hands
Still in prayer, otherwise moving:
>   Capable, crafting,
Showing their age, their years of usefulness
Giving expression to spirit,
I am she.

I am great mystery, unknown.
      I am Sophia, wisdom teacher.
      I am Minerva, warrior, crafter.
      Isis, lover, and Hecate, elder,
Goddess mother of all:
I am she.

Alphabetical List of First Lines

About The Author

Elizabeth Carson lives and writes in Victoria, British Columbia.

To learn more about her life and work, please visit lizanncarson.com.

www.ingramcontent.com/pod-product-compliance
Lightning Source LLC
Chambersburg PA
CBHW031628040426
42452CB00007B/736